CW01272518

Gin Shed 22

TAKE 8 GINS

Lorraine Isgrove

First published in the United Kingdom in 2018

ISBN: 9781730786990

Imprint: Independently published

Purple Marketing Scotland

www.purplemarketing.biz

Copyright © Lorraine Isgrove, 2018

The authors' moral rights have been asserted.

All rights reserved. No part of this publication may be reproduced, stored or transmitted in any form, or by any means electronic, mechanical or photocopying, recording or otherwise, without the express permission of the publisher.

Dedicated

To

The Ladies of the Shed

May the gin and banter always flow!

Press for Gin

Contents

About this little book	7
Cocktail Equipment	8
A note about Glassware	9
The Gins	10
The Martini	13
Gin & Tonic Collection	31
A Mix of Cocktails	49
Recipes for stuff	67
The Secret World of Gin Shed 22	77
Acknowledgements	79
Index	80

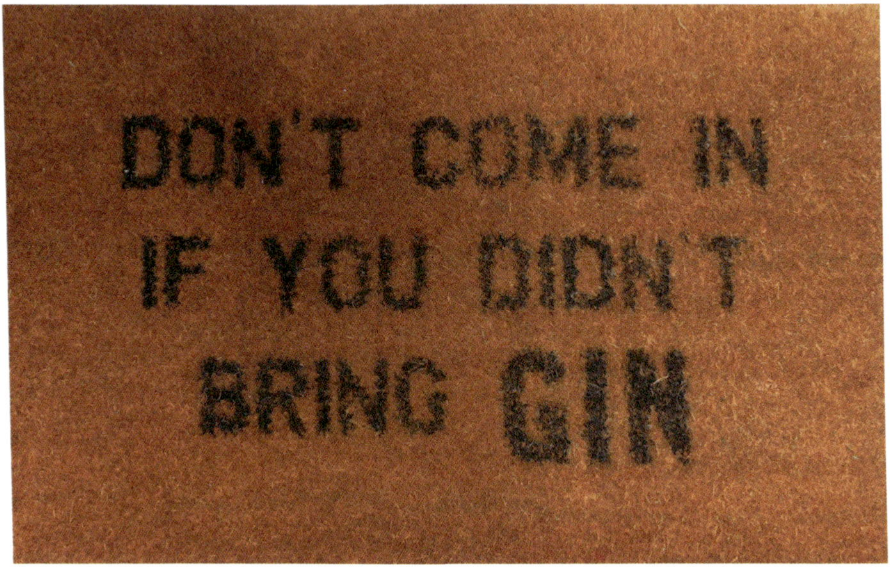
DON'T COME IN
IF YOU DIDN'T
BRING GIN

About this little book

Welcome to the inside of the gin shed, a place where women meet and men don't dare to enter. My name is Lorraine and I am the proud owner of the shed and author of this book.

This little book contains some of our favourite drinks from Gin Shed 22. Some of them are just great Gin & Tonics, others are one off experiments, but my favourites are the Martinis.

I have tried to keep the number of gins and ingredients to a minimum and reuse were possible, this is what you call a beginners guide to gin and cocktails. I have picked eight gins – very different from each other and at a variety of prices, but all readily available. I have put together three different ways to drink each one – a Martini, a G&T and a Cocktail. There are also a couple of recipes at the back to make your own infused gins, some basic syrups or even a liqueur.

It is just a bit of fun, the gins have been chosen purely on basis that we had them in the shed, we are not endorsing the brands, nor have we been asked to include a particular gin or brand. The tipsy comments are from the ladies of the shed, personal views and not expert tasting notes.

You can follow me on YouTube – Gin Shed 22 - to watch how to make some of the drinks and see inside the actual shed.

From all of us in the shed – we hope you enjoy making and drinking (responsibly) our gin cocktails.

Cocktail Equipment

It's important to have some bar equipment but you don't need to spend a fortune. You can buy shaker and measure sets from well known online shops that won't break the bank.

As a minimum you should have:

- A cocktail shaker
- Bar spoon
- Strainer or sieve
- 25ml & 50ml measures
- A nice martini jug for stirring without shaking
- Sharp knife
- Potato peeler or citrus zester

"You should always measure your ingredients – you can put in as many measures as you like – but at least you'll know how many you have had!"

A note about Glassware

How you serve your gin can be as important as how you prepare it. However, you don't have to spend a fortune to build up a selection of glasses.

Most of the glassware featured in the drinks pictures has come from antique centres or charity shops. They vary in price from 50p to £10 and can be brand new or as old as the Queen.

Have a hunt about, you don't have to have a matching set when making cocktails for friends but you can find some stunning glass sets for under £10 in your local charity shop.

"If you are a spiller – don't use a wide necked cocktail glass – get a Sippy cup"

The Gins

We have had probably around 50 different gins in the shed at one time or another. I think we have around 30 bottles currently with gin still in them. This wee book is about 8 of them - all very different in style.

- **Boë Violet Gin, 50cl 41.5% abv.**
    - Made by a local producer in Throsk in Stirling. Boë first appeared on the market in Spring 2017 readily available in Morrison's and independents. Light purple in colour and infused with violets to give a sweet perfume scent and flavour.

- **Bombay Sapphire Gin, 70cl 40% abv.**
    - Owned by Bacardi and made in Hampshire. Available worldwide, first appeared on the market in 1987 in its iconic blue bottle. A vapour infused gin using 10 botanicals, eight of which are used in the original Bombay Dry Gin recipe from 1761.

- **Brockmans Gin, 70cl 40% abv.**
    - In a stunning dark and mysterious bottle, Brockmans Gin first appeared in 2010 and is produced at G&J Distillers in Warrington. This is a dark fruits (clear) gin with not much of a juniper aroma or taste. However that does make it a favourite with the "I don't like gin" crowd and very easy to drink.

- **Hortus Citrus Garden Gin, 70cl 40% abv.**
    - Available throughout the summer months from Lidl, the limited edition own brand first appeared in June 2017. It is a pretty decent citrusy gin, cheap compared to others on the market and just as good.

- **Opihr Dry Gin, 70cl 40% abv.**
    - Made by G&J Distillery in Warrington, Opihr (o-peer) was launched in 2013. Hand picked spices selected from countries along the ancient Spice Route are infused into a high quality grain spirit, to produce a spicy new twist in the gin market.

Pink Gin, 50-70cl 37.5% and above abv.

- This is a particularly crowded area of the gin market, with varieties from all corners of the world. Pinkster raspberry Gin was one of the first launched in 2013 and has been quickly followed with variations from most of the large distilleries. Gordon's and Greenhall do delicious budget versions, which can be found in most supermarkets. We love the Square Peg Pink Gin made in Dunbartonshire, a small batch locally made version. There is also a recipe at the back of the book to make your own version of pink fruit infused gin – and then make jam with the boozy leftover fruit.

Sloe Gin, 25% - 30% abv.

- More of a gin liqueur than a full strength gin and alcohol volume is dependant on the producer. Dry, sweet and tart on the tongue. You can make your own with the recipe supplied at the back or Gordon's, Sipsmith and Warner Edwards produce some delicious versions.

Tanqueray Flor De Sevilla Gin, 70cl 41.3% abv.

- New to the market in spring 2018, inspired by recipes from the archives and made in Leven near Edinburgh. Clear light orange in colour. Very strong on the nose of fresh cut tangerines. Fruity and bitter to taste.

The recipes that follow can be used with any other brands of gin, taste test your gin neat first to get an idea of which recipe would suit its botanicals the best.

GIN
SHED
martini
G&T
22
recipe
shaker
drink
friends
fruit
cocktails
tonic
mix
ice
stir
chat
lemon
lime
gin
LADIES
shed
garnish
tonic

The Martini

Don't you just love a gin martini – dry, dirty, sweet, coffee or with anything you can find to make something strong, chilled and smooth. You can find martini recipes anywhere on the Internet, all using a combination of a base spirit and botanicals.

Essentially a classic gin martini is made with gin and dry Vermouth, the ratio of which is always up for debate.

There are four classic terms used to describe a Martini:

- Dry – little or no dry Vermouth
- Wet – equal parts gin and Vermouth
- Perfect – use both dry and sweet Vermouth
- Dirty – add a little brine from the olive jar

Then there is the method – shaken or stirred? My preference is stirred - over lots of ice - to chill thoroughly, stirring for a minimum of 30 seconds. You are looking to dilute the spirit by around 30% with iced water.

Pouring the martini into a chilled glass will complete the ceremony, before adding the appropriate garnish of choice.

We obviously like the gin based martini cocktails in the shed and have put together some of our favourite combinations.

"I like to have a martini, two at the very most.
After three I'm under the table, after four I'm under my host."
Dorothy Parker

Classic Martini

A classic martini is made from a good quality gin and vermouth. The better the gin the smoother the martini. For me; a martini is basically gin over ice with the ice removed.

Ingredients:

- 60ml Brockmans gin
- Vermouth to taste
- Lemon or lime zest twist

Method:

Fill a shaker or tall glass with ice and add gin and vermouth. Alternatively use the vermouth to swish around the glass and then throw away. Stir for at least 30 seconds to chill the alcohol and dilute with iced water – around 30% dilution.

Chill a martini glass with ice before straining the martini into it and garnishing. Sip slowly savouring the delicious dark forest fruits.

"A perfect Martini should be made by filling a glass with gin, then waving it in the general direction of Italy"
Noel Coward (who unfortunately never made it to the shed)

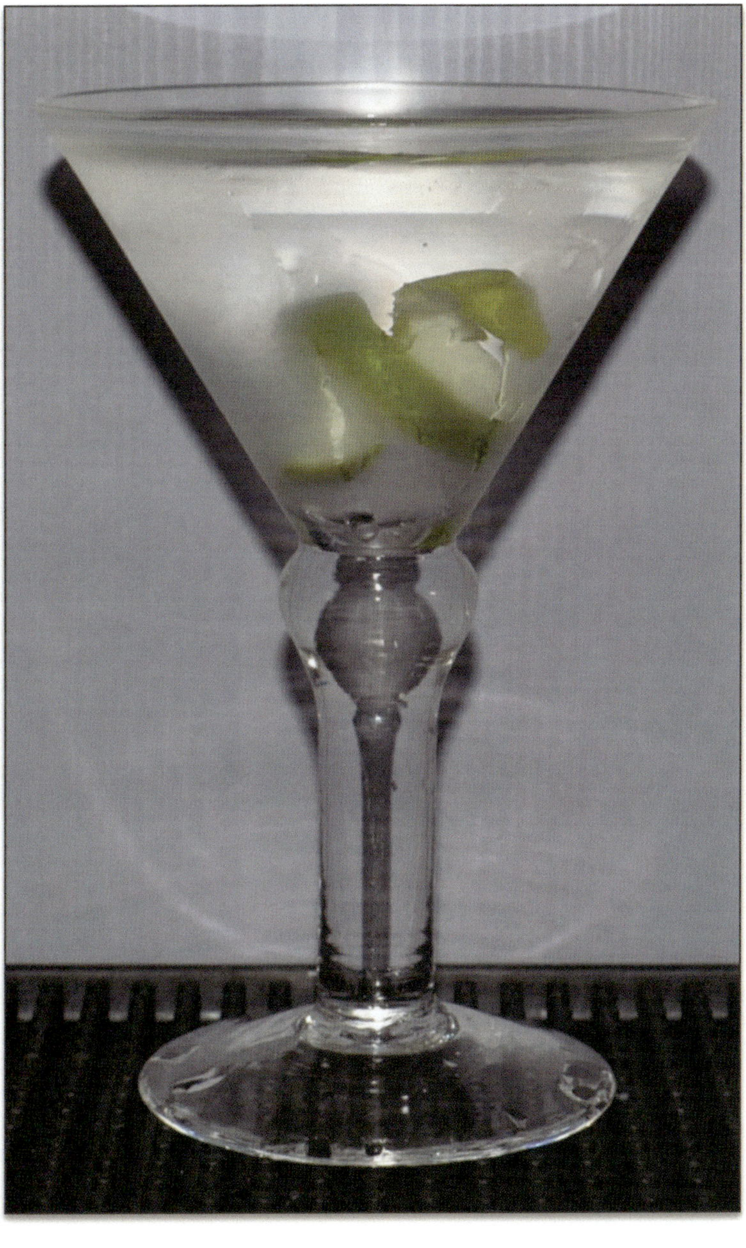

Dirty Martini

This works best with a very smooth slightly spiced gin. The salt from the olives combines with a bit of chilli or pepper from the gin, in the most moreish way. Warning can be addictive.

Ingredients:

- 60ml of Opihr gin
- 1tsp. of brine from the olive jar
- 5 green olives
- Lots of ice
- Chilled martini glass

Method:

Add all the ingredients apart from three olives into a jug or tall glass and muddle the olives until they break up slightly. Continuing stirring and mixing until the ice has melted approximately 20ml of water into the gin. Double strain into a chilled martini glass and garnish with the remaining olives.

"My new favourite gin for this martini - spicy"

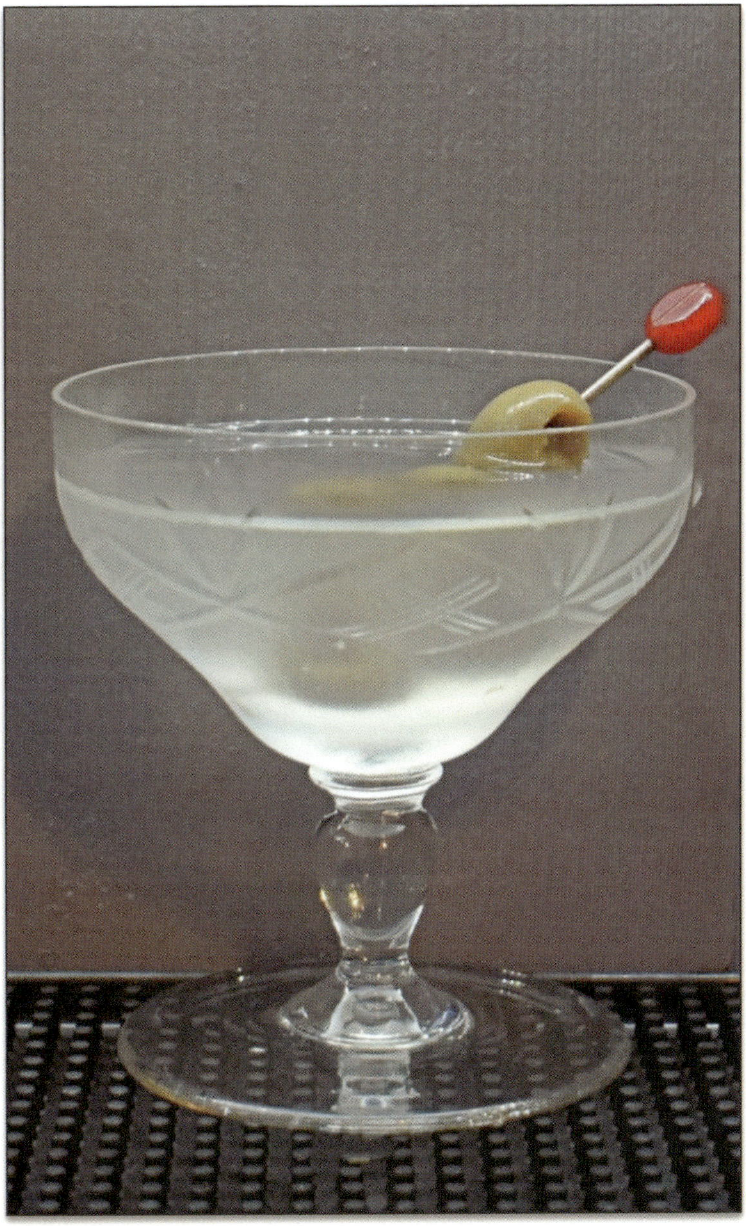

Pink Martini

There are loads of amazing pink gins out there and this is definitely one for the summer. You can make your own pink gin using raspberries, strawberries or cranberries – there is a recipe at the back of the book.

Ingredients:

- 60ml of Pink gin (Gordon's do a great one)
- 15ml of fresh lemon juice
- A slice of lemon
- Lots of ice

Method:

Fill a shaker or tall glass with ice, add the gin and lemon juice. Stir for at lest 30 seconds to chill the alcohol and dilute with iced water – around 30% dilution.

Chill a martini glass with ice before straining the martini into it and garnishing it with the lemon slice. Sip slowly savouring the delicious light summery fruit flavour.

"This is an incredibly easy to drink – any more than 3 – well who knows what will happen"

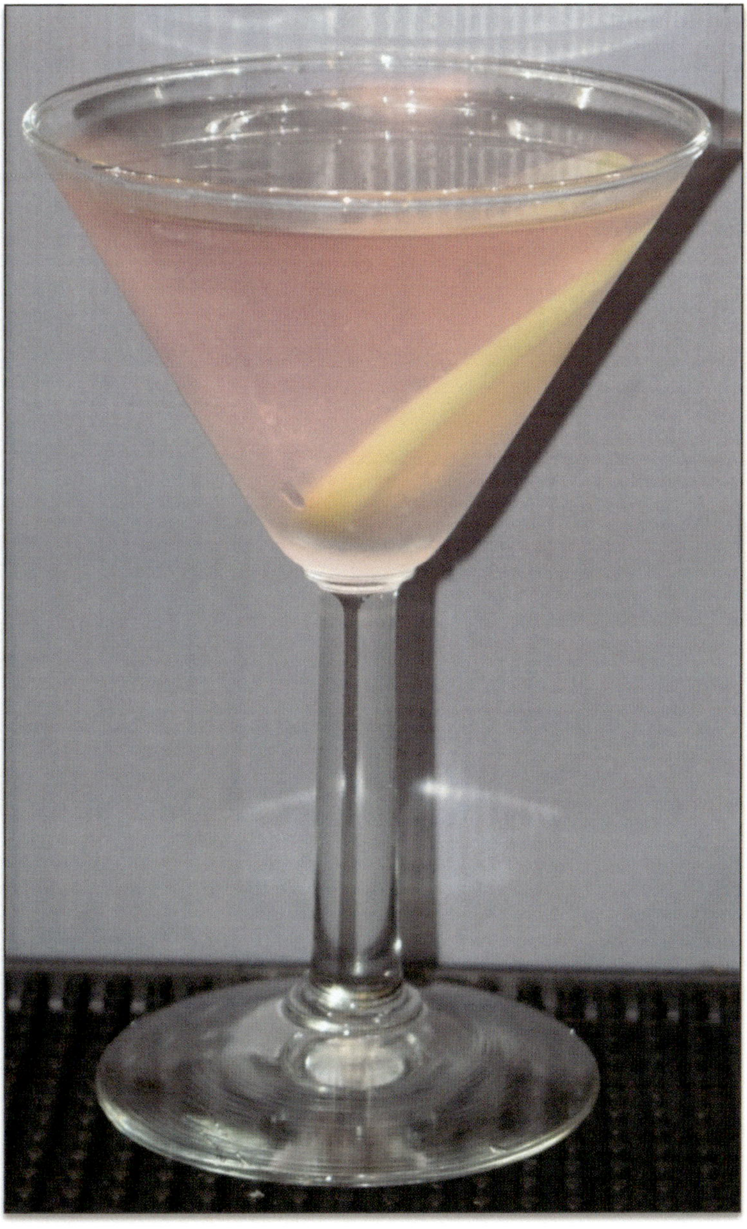

Fig Martini

A sweet and tangy martini, ideal with an Italian meat or cheese board. Recipe for the fig syrup is at the back of the book. Alternatively you could use a raspberry or strawberry puree.

Ingredients:

- 60ml of Bombay Sapphire gin
- 20ml of fresh fig syrup
- 10ml of fresh lemon juice
- A slice of fresh fig

Method:

Fill a shaker with ice then add the gin and fig syrup. Shake for at lest 30 seconds until the shaker is cold to touch on the outside.

Chill a martini glass with ice before straining the martini into it and garnishing. Enjoy with a delicious array of savoury snacks.

"Something different — the fig really works with the gin - yummy"

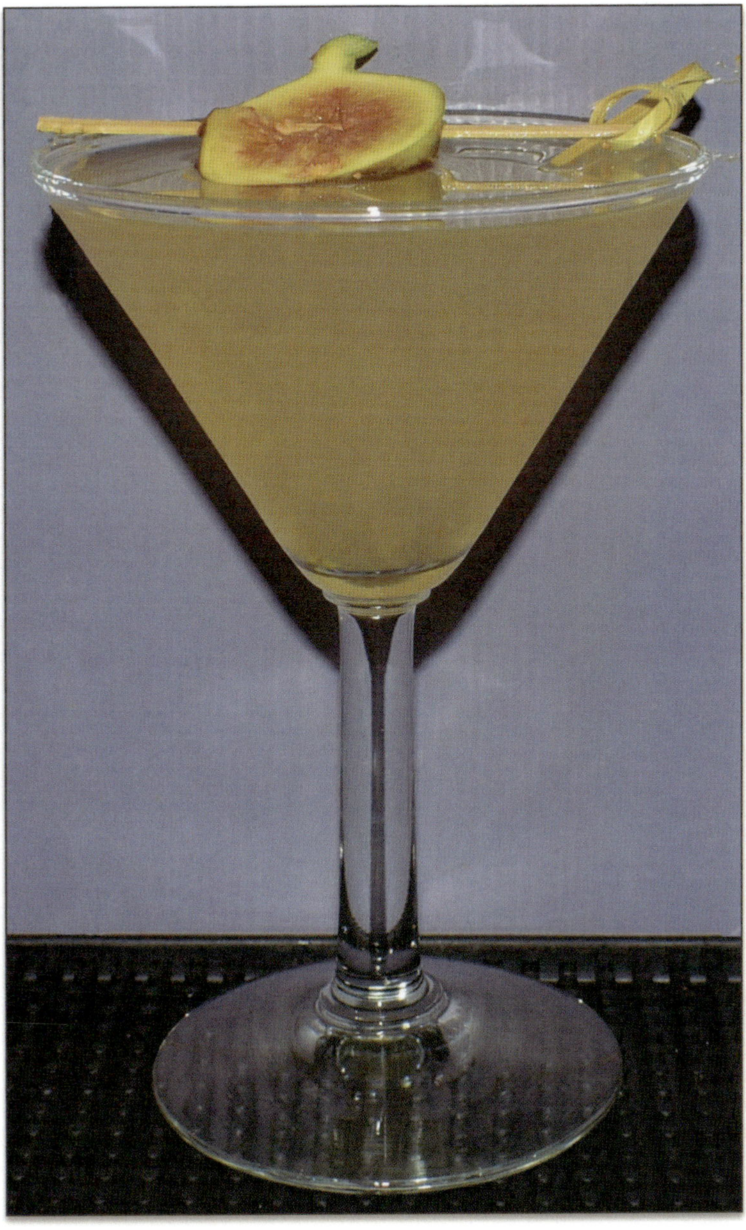

The Aviation

Is it a martini? – At a pinch – it's small, very alcoholic and cold so fits the bill in my book. Plus it's purple.

Ingredients:

- 60ml Boë Violet gin
- 20ml fresh lemon juice
- 10ml Maraschino liqueur

Method:

Again as in previous martini recipes, place in shaker filled with ice and stir to mix and chill. Pour into a small cocktail or martini glass and garnish with a maraschino cherry.

If you can't get Boe Violet then replace with a good dry gin and add 10 ml of Crème de Violette.

Maraschino liqueur can be expensive to purchase if only using for this one cocktail, so we cheat in the gin shed and use the maraschino cherry juice from the jar instead.

"This one can actually make you fly and dance to ABBA with the dog"

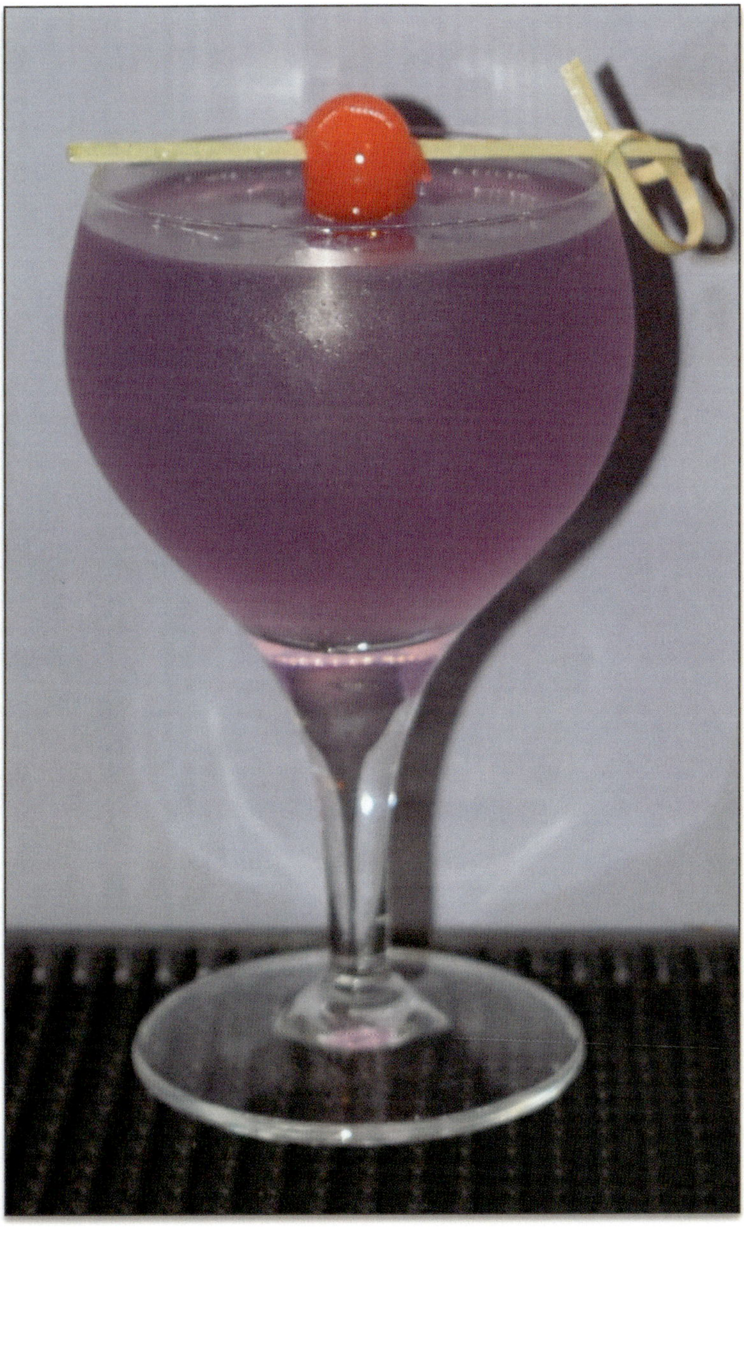

Perfectly Sloe Martini

This is a lush deep tasting martini with hints of Christmas; make your own sloe gin for best results. We served this up with some baked feta cheese with honey & Thyme.

Ingredients:

- 40ml Sloe gin
- 20ml Dry Vermouth
- 20ml Sweet Vermouth
- Lots of ice
- Lemon zest twist to garnish

Method:

Put the gin and both Vermouths into a mixing glass or jug with the ice and stir for around 30 seconds.

Strain into a chilled cocktail glass and garnish with the lemon.

"Reminiscent of a chilled good quality port with hints of clover and cinnamon"

25

Breakfast Martini

When you can lounge around on a Sunday and not have to worry about driving that day. This is a perfect start to breakfast in bed with warm croissants and somebody to wait on you.

Ingredients:

- 50ml Tanqueray Flor De Sevilla gin
- 1 tbsp. lemon juice
- 1½ tsp. of orange marmalade
- Orange zest twist to garnish

Method:

Place the gin, lemon juice and marmalade into a cocktail shaker full of ice. Shake to mix thoroughly.

Pour into a chilled martini glass and add the orange zest twist to garnish.

"Not much will get done in a day if you have one of these for breakfast"

27

Gimlet

Not strictly a martini but again only two ingredients and it's chilled and strong. This drink can be quite tangy depending on the lime syrup mix. Spanish or Mexican tapas are an excellent accompaniment to citrus flavours.

Ingredients:

- 50ml of lime cordial or homemade lime syrup
- 50ml Hortus Citrus Garden gin
- Lot of ice
- Slice of lime to garnish

Method:

Add the gin and lime syrup or cordial into a jug or tall glass and add ice cubes. Stir, until the outside of the container feels very cold. Strain the mixture into a chilled martini glass and garnish with a slice of lime

Use 25 ml fresh lime juice and 25 ml simple syrup if you don't have lime cordial. Or make your own lime syrup - recipe at the back.

"Ooooh" "Liquid Porn"

29

G&T Collection

Gin & Tonic Collection

There is nothing nicer than sitting down to a perfectly balanced gin and tonic. Light fruity ones for the summer and spicy warming ones in the winter.

There is a long history to gin and tonic going back the 19th century and the British Army in India, server with ice and a slice. The Spanish however, have taken the G&T to a whole new level with the use of oversized balloon or coppa glasses filled with lots, and lots of ice and complimentary garnishes.

The ladies of the shed are somewhere between the ice and a slice G&T and a full on garnished one, it really depends on the gin and glass in use.

I have used a variety of glass styles, again depending on the gin used. What they all start with is lots of ice; freshly opened mixers and deliciously fresh garnish.

I have also included in this wee collection, is a couple of G&Ts using alternatives to tonic water, as sometimes it not always the best complement to the gin – in our opinion.

The wonderful thing about the gin explosion is the variety of mixers that are now available. The old days of Gordon's and Schweppes being the only choice have long gone, with all producers upping their game considerably. The sugar tax in the UK has also helped pushed the manufacturers to produce healthier versions, which are becoming more readily available. Favourites in the shed include Fever-Tree, Fentimens and the Tesco's own brand is quite decent as well.

If you have a lovely craft gin, get a lovely tonic to go with it. You don't want to overwhelm those carefully crafted botanicals. If you are really stuck with what goes with what, try the phone app Ginventory or look up the perfect serve on the gin brand website.

Again measure your gin; free pouring can ruin a great G&T by either being too strong or too weak. Work out your perfect ratio for the gin, in the shed we are between 1 part gin to 3 parts tonic unless it's a high abv. gin, then we put in more tonic – 1-4 ratio.

"When life hands you lemons, make a gin and tonic"
Anon

Classic Gin & Tonic

Everybody's go to in a bar, classic, timeless and easy to drink.

Ingredients:

- 50ml Bombay Sapphire gin
- 150ml Indian tonic water
- Lime wedge to garnish

Method:

Fill a tall glass with ice. Pour in the gin. Top up gently with tonic water stirring slightly to mix. Add lime the garnish.

"Refreshingly sharp – goes down too quickly"

"You are the gin to my tonic"

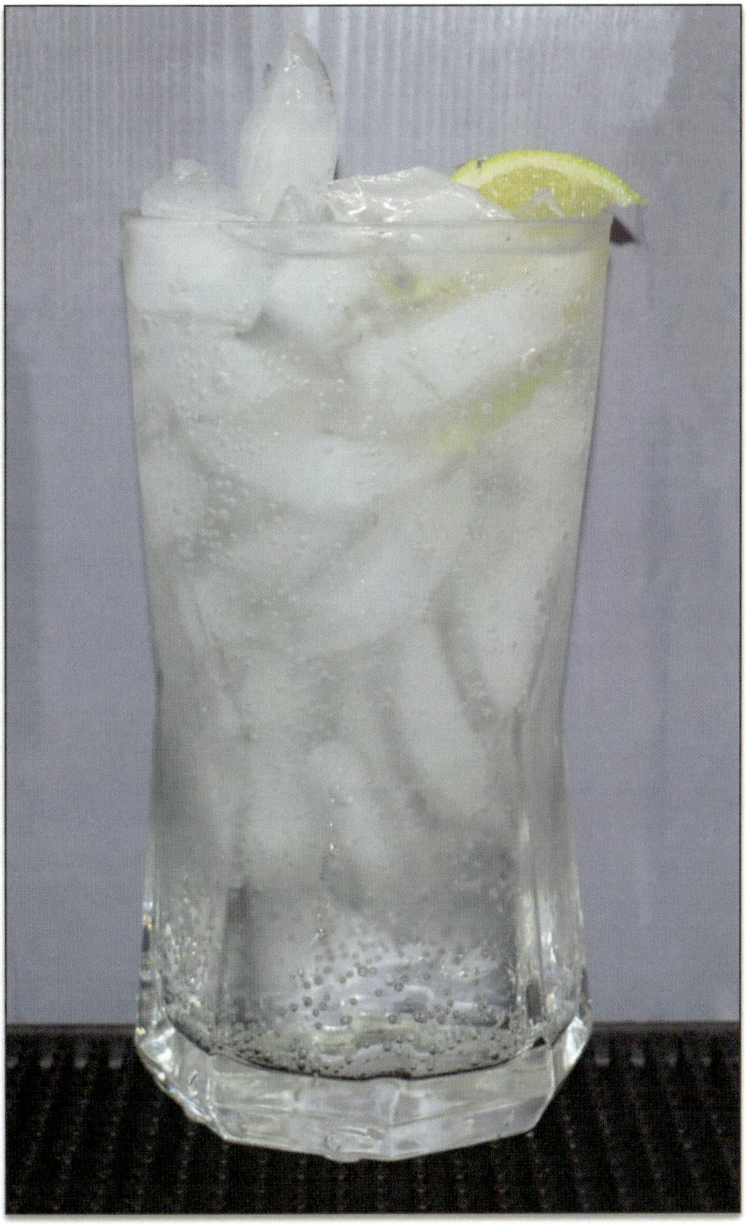

Pink Gin & Tonic

Pink gin is so versatile, it has an amazing summer fruits flavour that can be built on with either more floral notes or contrasted with citrus.

Ingredients:

- 50ml Pink gin (Square Peg Pink gin is delicious)
- 150ml elderflower tonic
- Pink fruit to garnish – strawberries or raspberries

Method:

Fill a coppa glass with lots of ice, pour over gin and top with the elderflower tonic. Stir gently to mix and garnish with fruit.

Tip: Buying mixed frozen berries from the supermarket, keeps this drink in season all year round.

"Still a favourite in the shed – tastes like juice"

"I wasn't sure – but I love this"

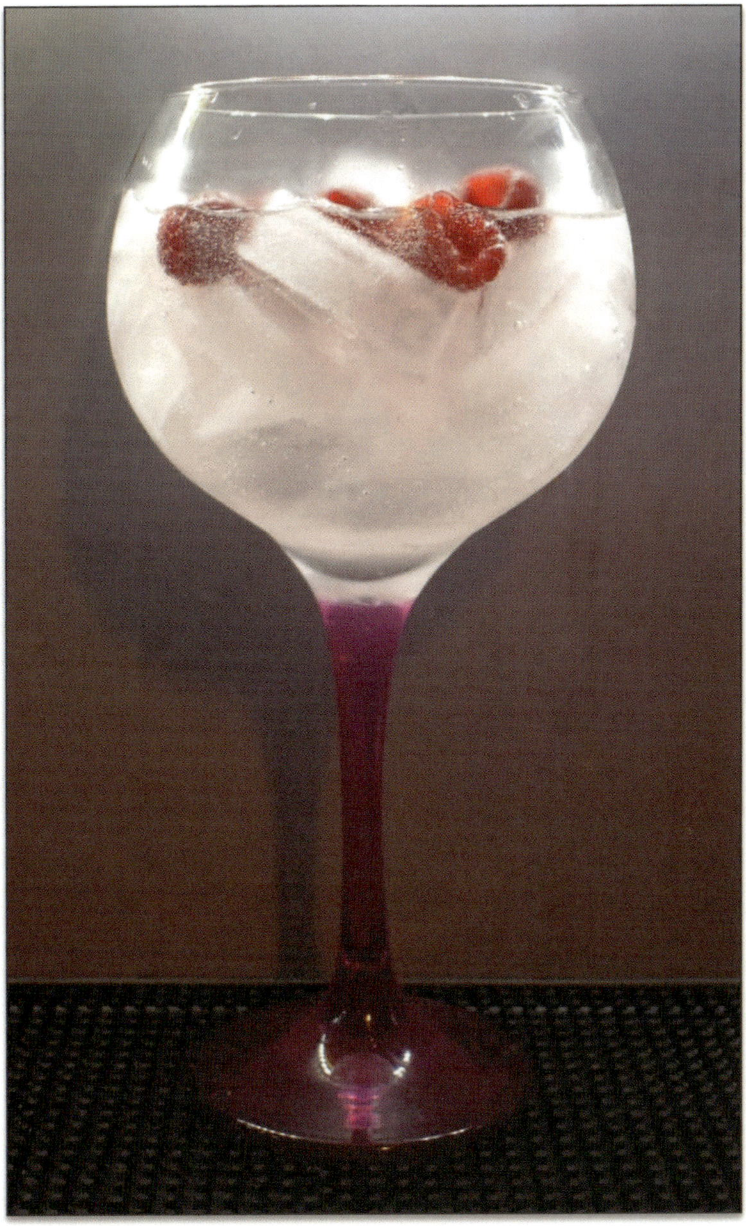

Citrus Gin Mojito

If you are not a fan of tonic then this recipe is a great alternative as it uses soda water instead.

Ingredients:

- 6-8 Mint leaves
- 40ml of Hortus Citrus Garden gin
- 20ml Fresh lemon juice
- 15ml Of simple syrup
- Soda water
- Slice of lime to garnish

Method:

Add lime juice, mint leaves and simple into a cocktail shaker and muddle (bash and mix) with a cocktail muddler or the end of a wooden spoon. Add the gin then pour into a glass filled with ice, leaving 2-3 cm of room. Top with soda water and garnish with more mint leaves and slice of lime.

"Summer in a glass – just needs a Caribbean beach to drink it on"

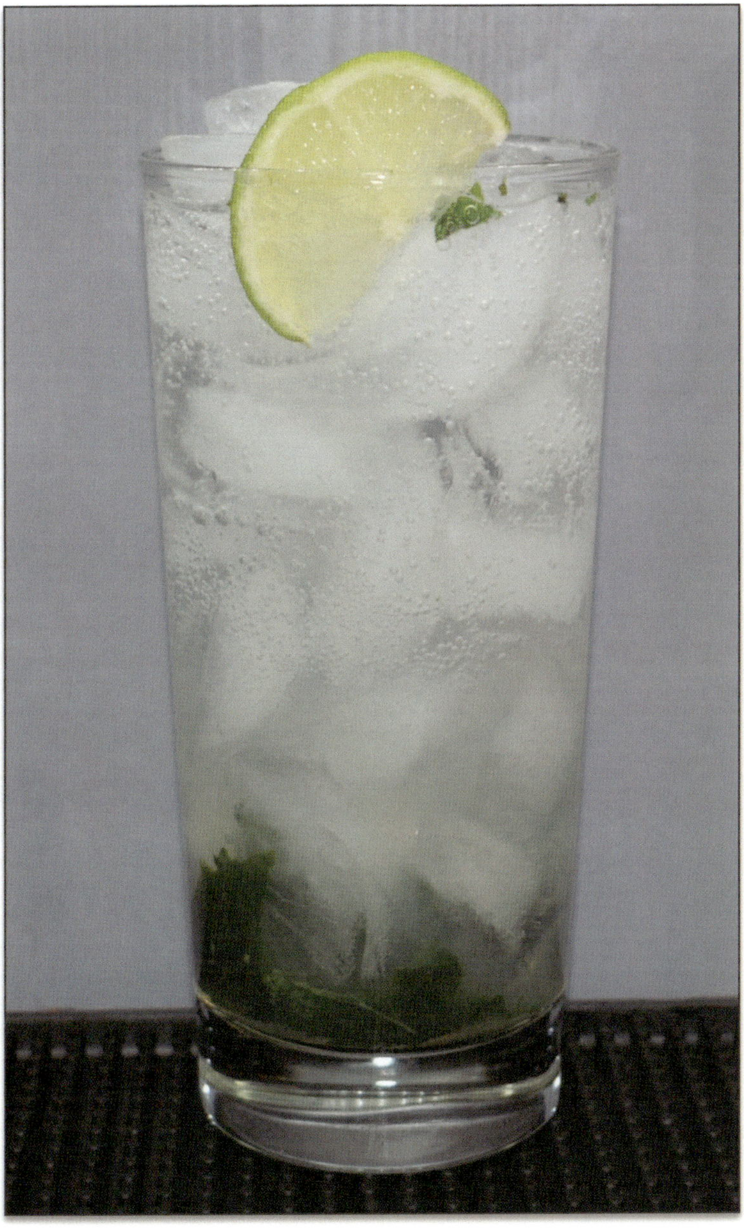

Purple & Sweet

We love a purple drink, luckily a local Distillery – Boë, makes a fabulous Violet gin. This can be quite sweet so a lemon tonic goes well to help balance it out.

Ingredients:

- 50ml Boë Violet gin
- 150ml lemon tonic water
- Grapefruit zest twist to garnish

Method:

Fill a coppa glass with ice. Pour in the gin.

Top up gently with lemon tonic water stirring slightly to mix. Add grapefruit twist the garnish.

If can't get a hold of Boe Violet gin, then using a good quality dry gin and adding 20 ml Crème de Violet liqueur will give you similar results – just a bit more alcoholic.

"Mmmmm – I do like that a lot"

"Purple gin & tonic – almost perfect"

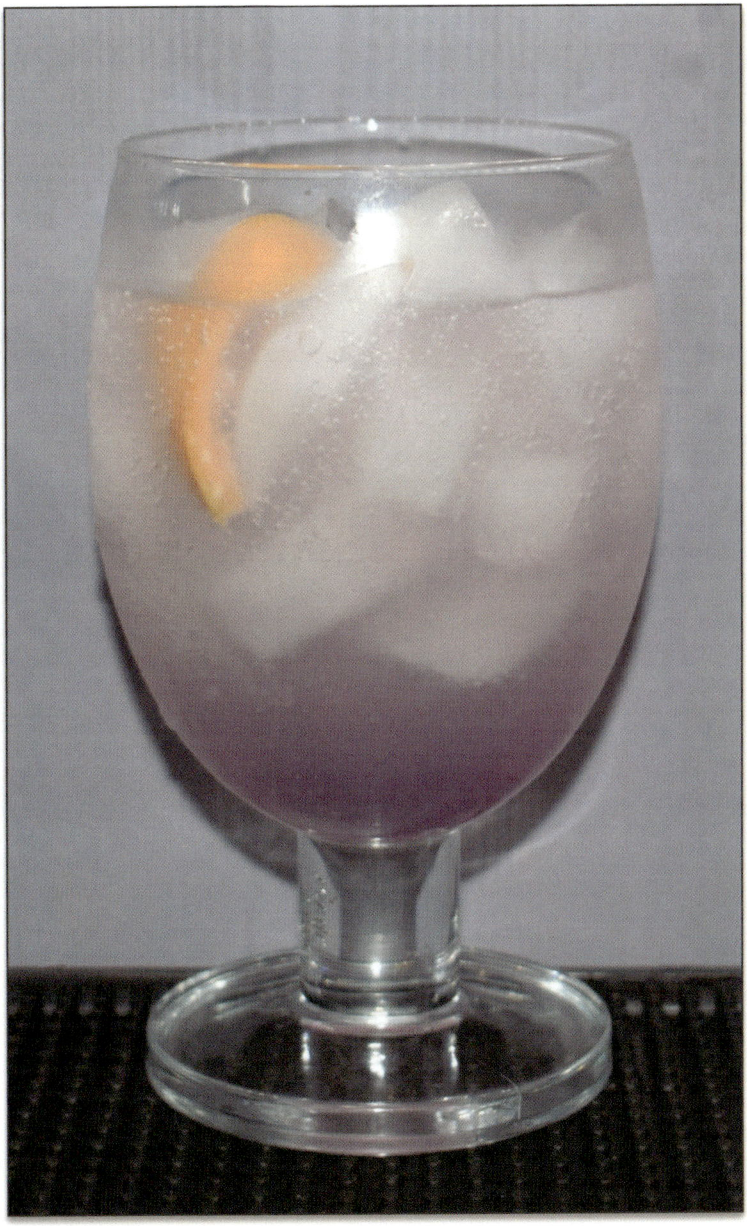

Autumn Fruits

This is just a great gin and tonic, it is easy to drink – some might say too easy – it always surprises you with it delicious fruity flavour and it loved by all of us in the shed.

Ingredients:

- 50ml Brockmans gin
- 150ml light tonic water
- Lots of ice
- Orange zest twist and blueberries to garnish

Method:

Fill a tall glass ¾ of the way with ice and add the gin. Top with tonic and gently mix with a long bar spoon. Garnish with the fruit.

"Ooh I do like a Brockmans, you can't get it wrong"

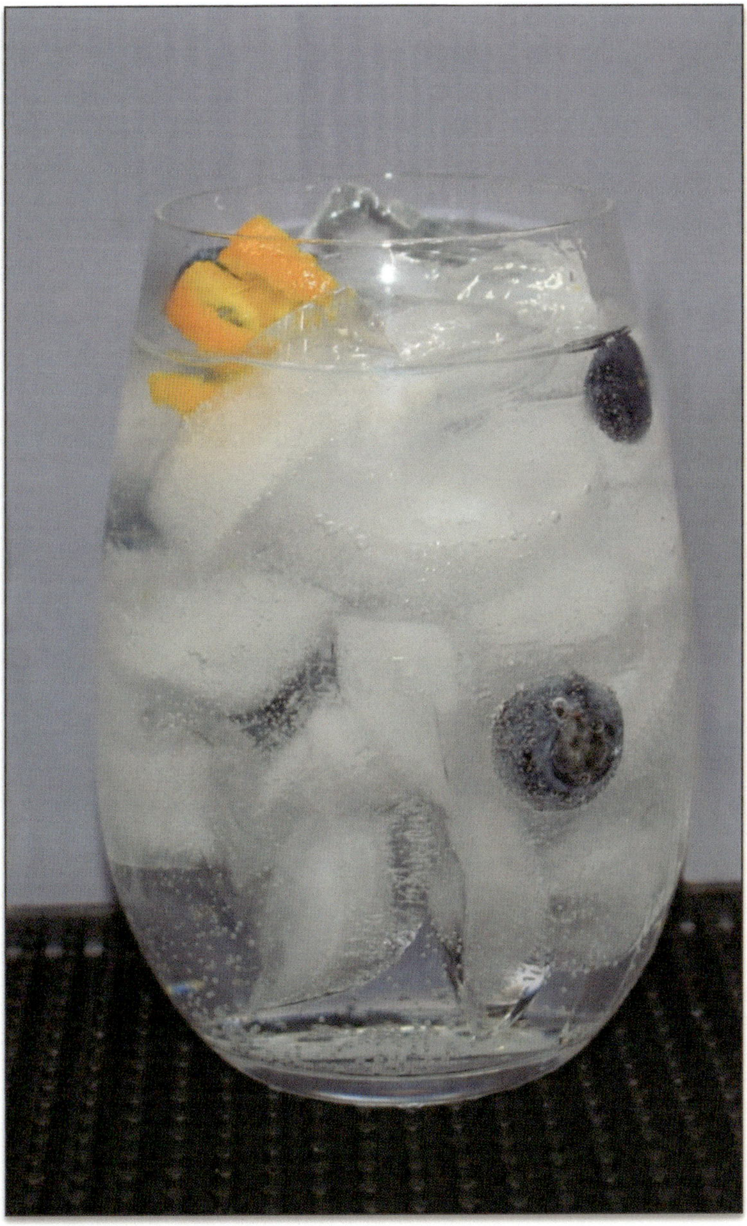

Tangy Gin & Tonic

For something slightly different and with a great citrus tang, this gin and tonic offers a refreshing change from the slightly sweeter gins.

Ingredients:

- 50ml Tanqueray Flor De Sevilla gin
- 150ml premium Indian tonic
- A squeeze of fresh orange juice
- Orange zest twist to garnish
- Lots of ice

Method:

Fill a large coppa glass with ice, add the gin and a squeeze of orange juice and mix gently. Top with tonic and finish with the twist of orange zest.

"Spain in a glass"

"Light, refreshing, cleanses the palate"

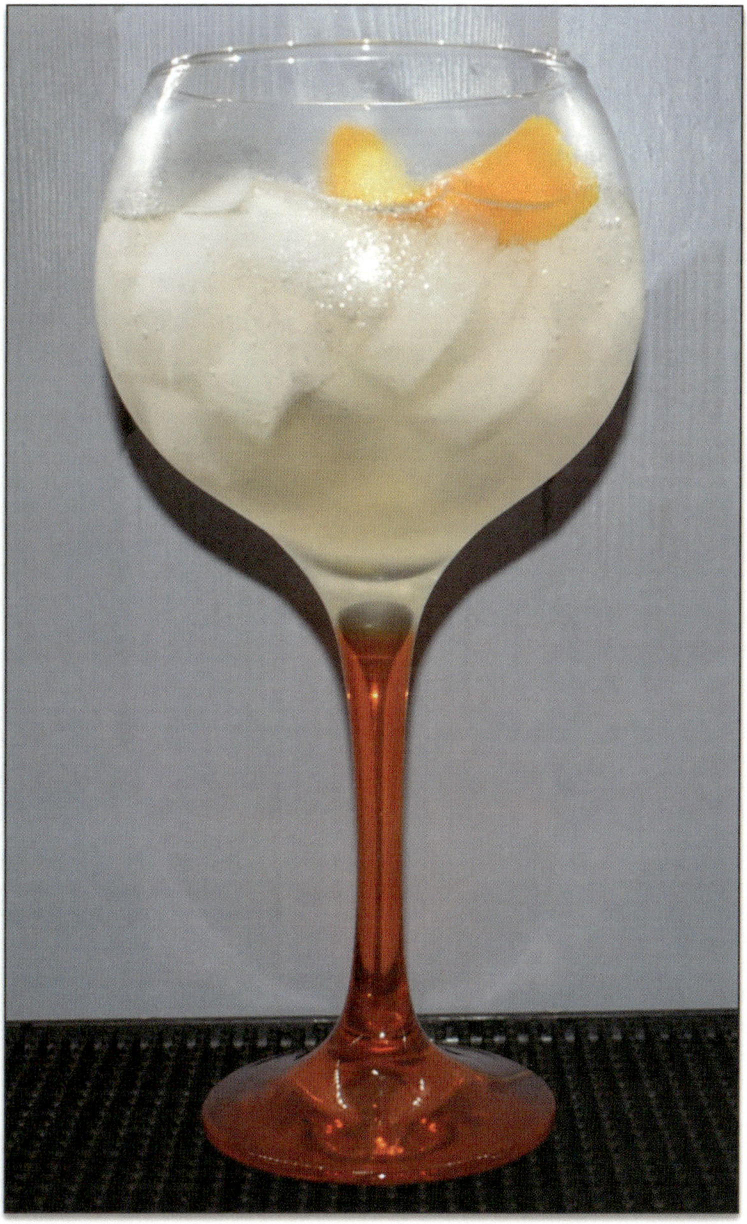

Sloe Gin & Tonic

Something for winter with the lemon tonic lifting the dryness and sweetness of the Sloe gin. Most Sloe gins are liqueurs so the lemon helps add some sourness.

Ingredients:

- 50 ml Sloe gin
- 150 ml lemon tonic water
- Lemon wedge to garnish

Method:

Fill a tall glass with ice. Pour in the gin.

Top up gently with the lemon tonic water stirring slightly to mix. Add lemon to garnish.

If you are feeling adventurous, there is a Sloe gin recipe at the back of the book. By making your own, you can control the amount of sugar added to the gin, making it more versatile. You can always add simple syrup to your drink if you need more sweetness.

"Dark fruits with an after tang"

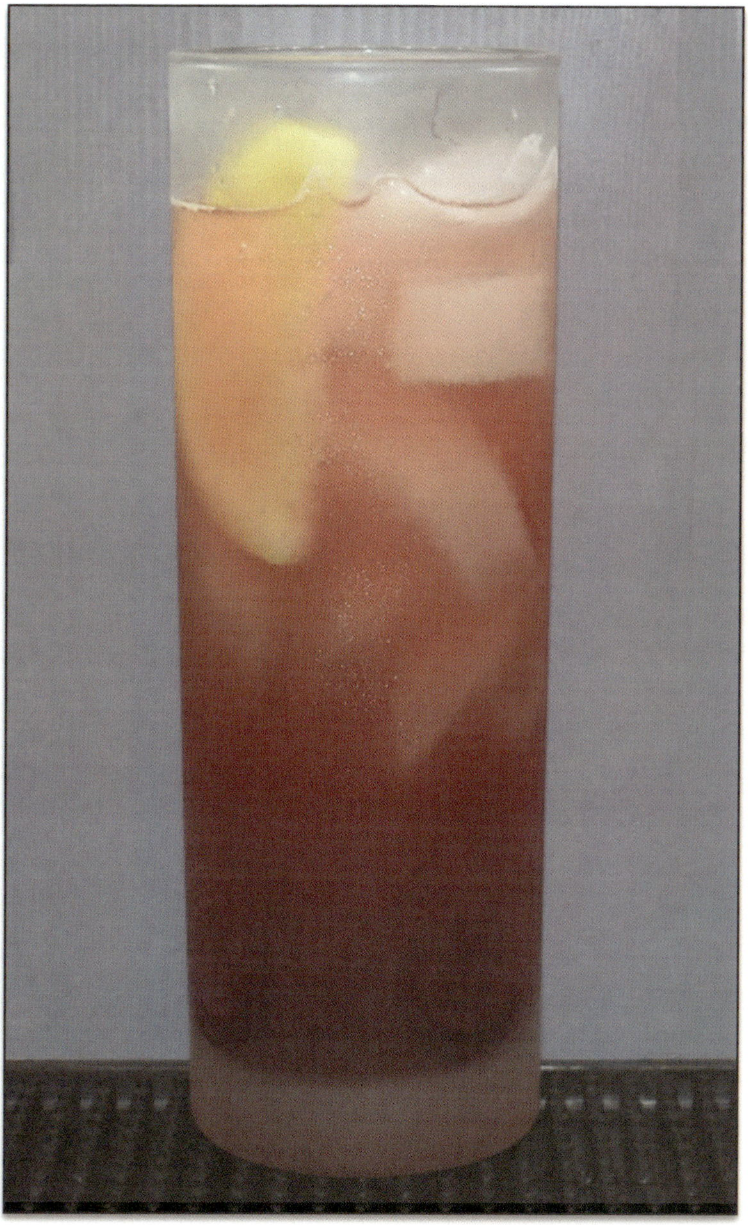

Spicy Nights

This is a great savoury spicy gin, very smooth with a nice bite to the taste. Brilliant with savoury foods like Indian takeaways or Thai curry.

Ingredients:

- 50ml of Opihr gin
- 150ml premium Indian tonic
- Lots of ice
- Slice of fresh ginger

Method:

Fill a large coppa glass with ice, and add the gin. Top with tonic and finish with the slice of ginger.

"Strong & spicy – how I like my men"

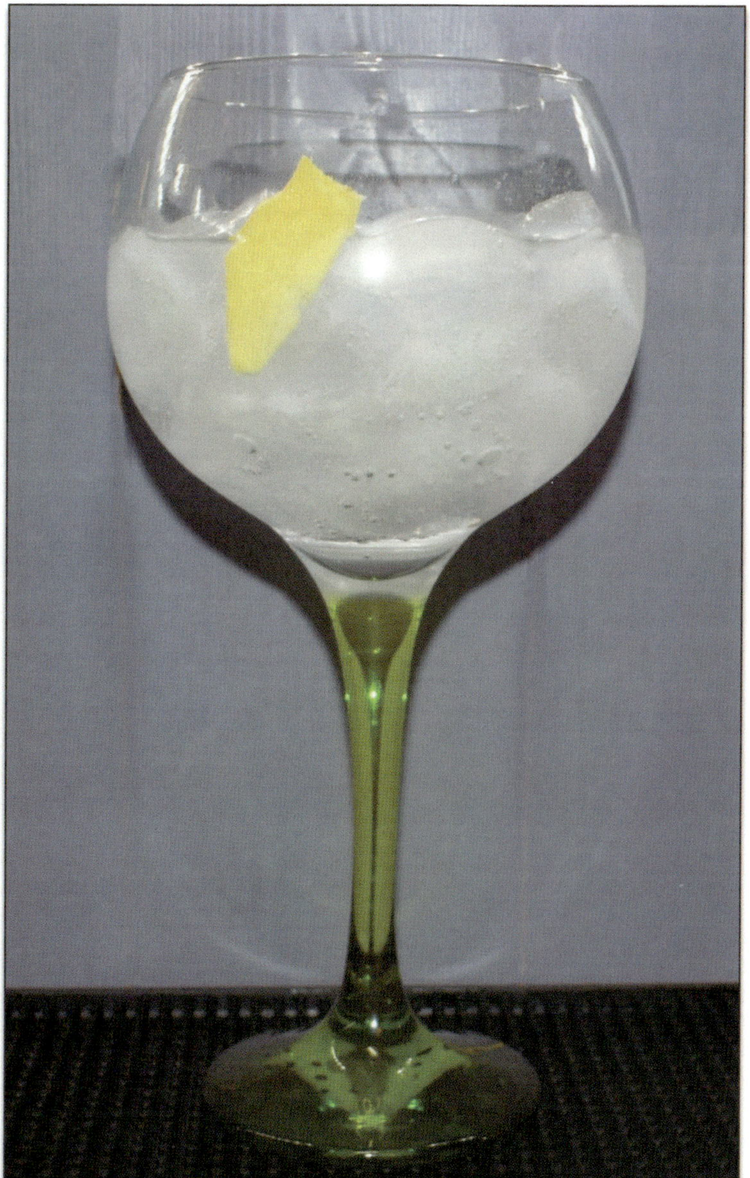

48

A Mix of Cocktails

So what is a cocktail? Anything you want it to be would be the simple answer, but it is mainly a drink containing one or more spirits mixed with other ingredients such as juices or syrups. They can be simple, with a combination of 3 perfectly balanced ingredients or more complex with outlandish botanicals and syrups not readily available for the home bar.

Like baking and cooking it's all in the ingredients, the quantity and the quality of them. Adding too much citrus can over power the drink, but adding too little leaves your cocktail sickly sweet.

There are many types of cocktails, shorts, longs, fizzy, frothy, sweet sour, usually chilled but can be served warm. Finding cocktails that you enjoy can be daunting, especially when looking at a bar menu of exotic combinations, which are not cheap.

Start at home with some easy cocktails from this book, from there you can get a better understanding of what flavour profiles you enjoy the most.

We love a good cocktail in the shed, it mixes things up and gives us a chance to experiment with a new gin. We never have more than one or two as it can all get a bit messy and someone has to wash up all the glasses in the morning.

"It's never too early for a cocktail"

Noel Coward

Floradora

Ingredients:

- 40ml Pink gin
- 20ml lime juice
- 10ml raspberry syrup
- Ginger beer
- Lime and raspberries to garnish

Method:

Add the gin, lime juice and raspberry syrup to a highball glass filled with ice. Stir lightly to mix then top with ginger beer. Garnish with the raspberries and lime slice.

"Reminds me of a previous era – flapper girls and all that"

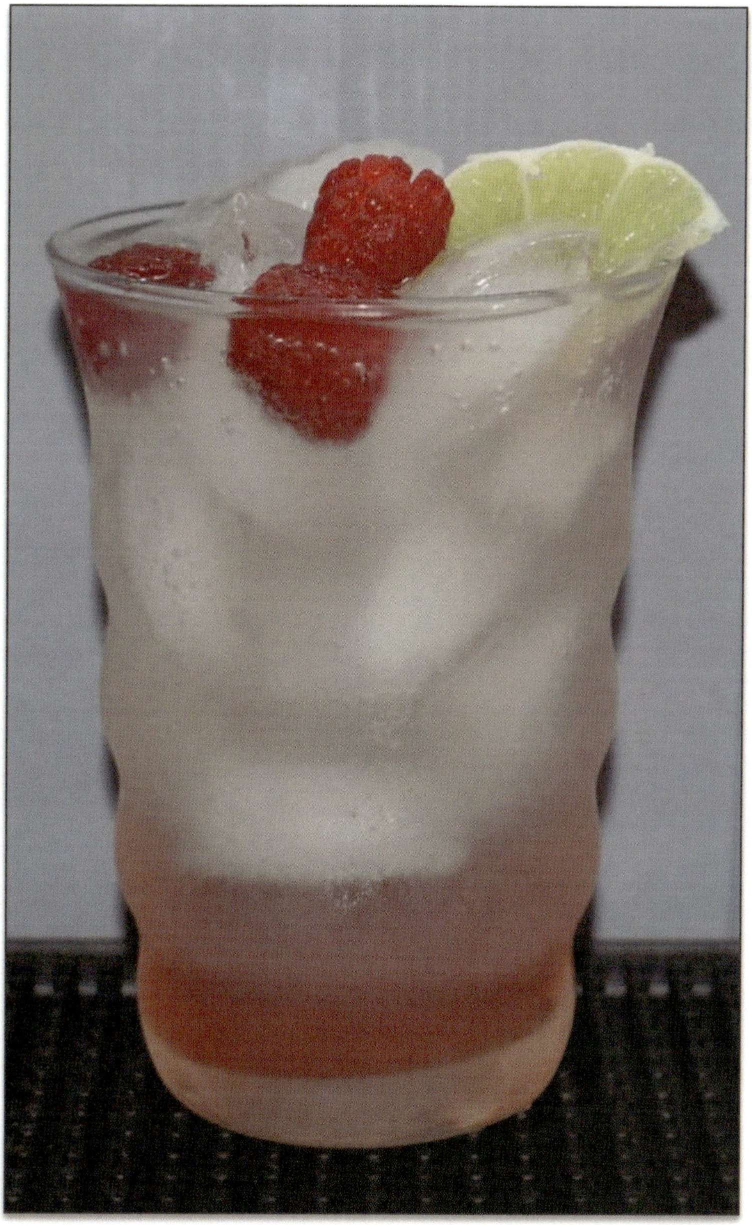

Spanish Cosmo

A tangy sweet short drink, in a beautiful shade of pink. Perfect as summers evening cocktail while catching up on the gossip.

Ingredients:

- 30ml of Tanqueray Flor De Sevilla gin
- 25ml cranberry juice
- 15ml Triple Sec
- 10ml freshly squeezed lime juice

Method:

Add all the ingredients into a cocktail shaker with lots of ice and shale for 30 seconds.

Pour into a chilled martini or champagne coupe glass.

"Not one you could have a lot of, but love the sweet sour contrast"

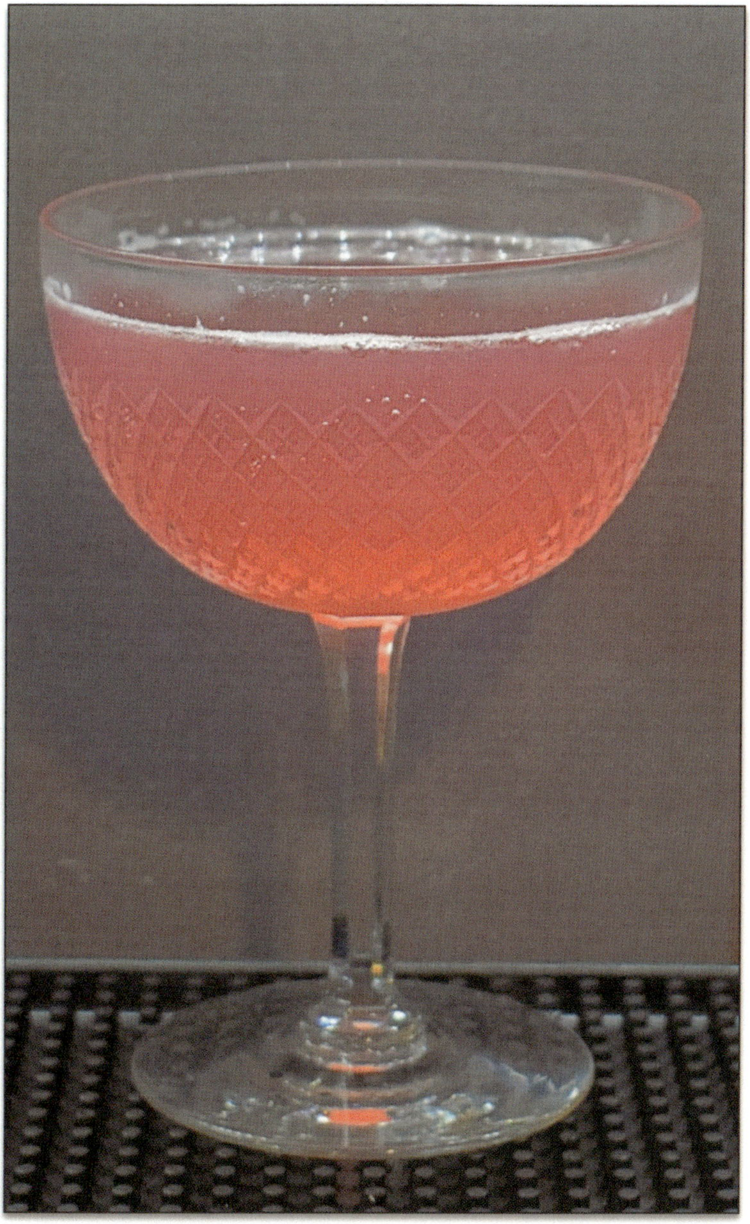

Sloe Royale

A celebratory drink with a difference for the winter season, the combination of the sloe gin and champagne gives a dark fruity crisp finish.

Ingredients:

- 15ml Sloe gin
- 100ml Champagne
- Lemon zest twist - optional

Method:

Chill the Champagne flute, add the Sloe gin, top with champagne. Garnish with the lemon zest twist if desired.

Merry Christmas and Happy New Year.

"Even more liquid porn"

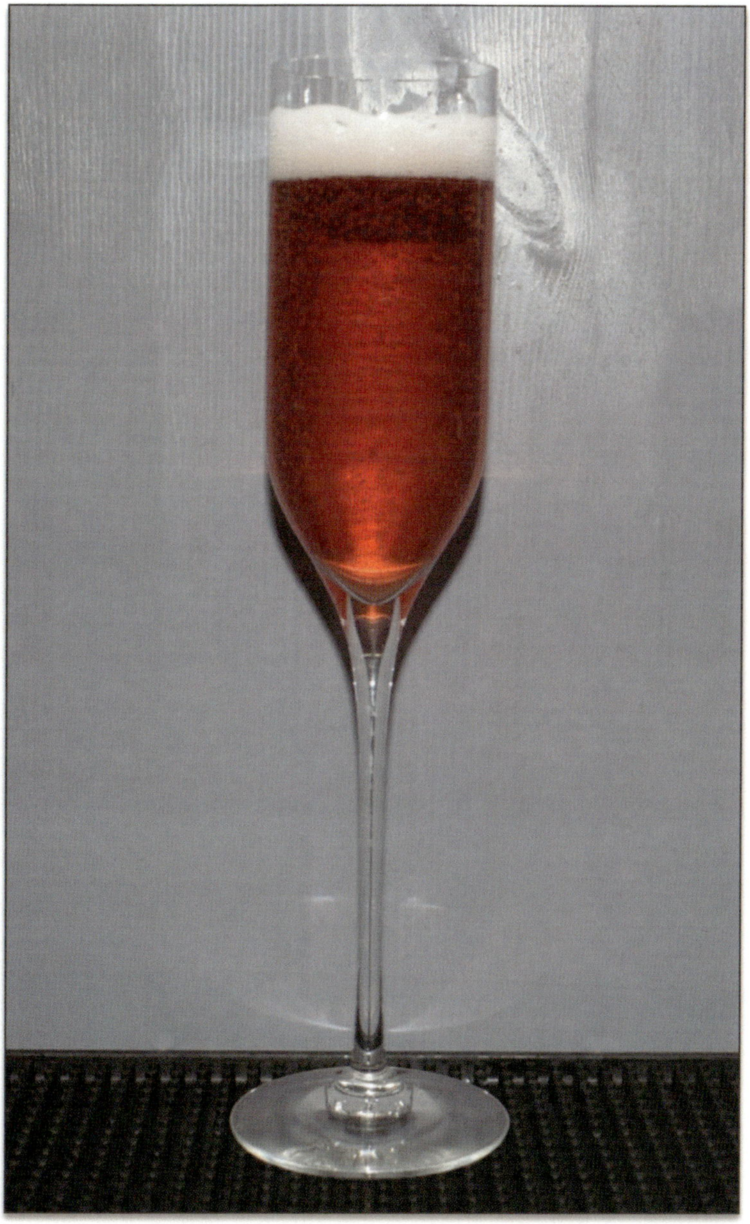

Gin Gin Mule

Like a Moscow Mule but with gin! An old recipe made great with the explosion of exotic gins. Great with spicy food or as a winter warmer.

Ingredients:

- 50ml of Opihr gin
- 15ml simple syrup
- 15ml lime juice
- 100ml ginger beer
- Mint leaves and slice of lime to garnish

Method:

Add the mint leaves to a tall glass and muddle to break up and release flavour. Add ice, gin, syrup and lime juice and mix gently. Top with ginger beer and garnish with the lime slice.

"Can it be spicy and refreshing?"

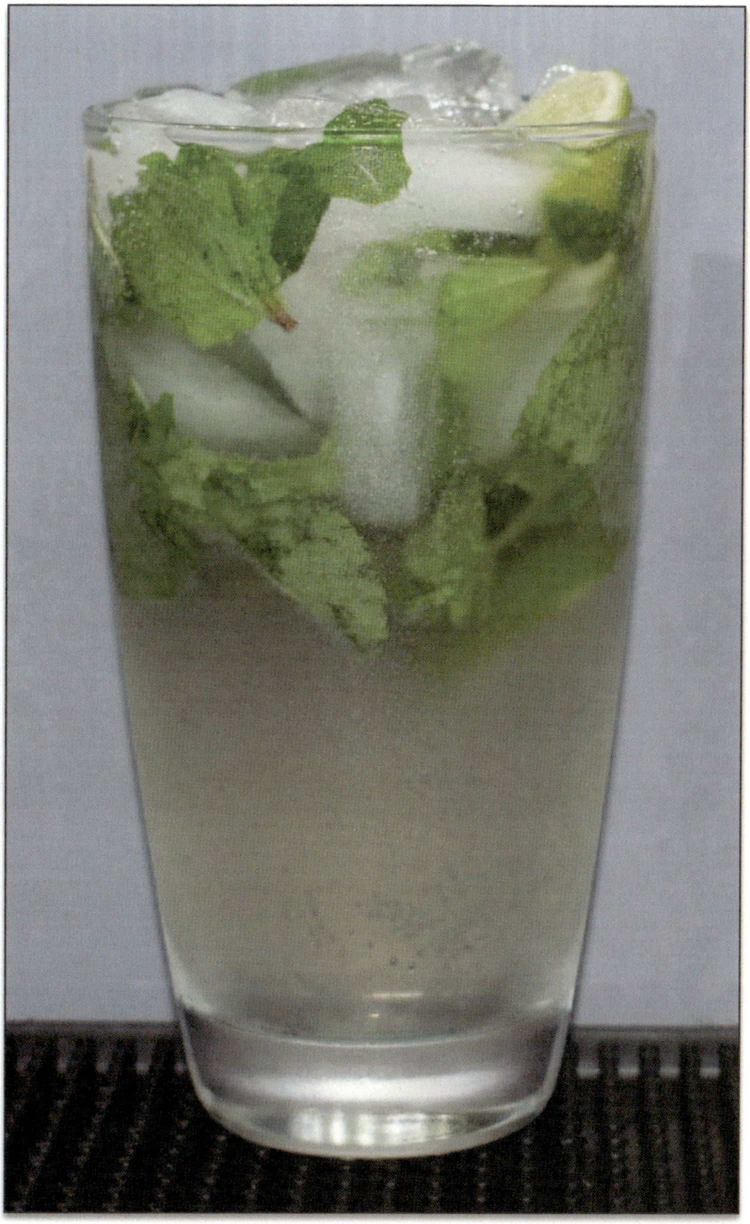

Blackberry Mule

A delicious mix of blackberry wine liqueur, gin and lime. Something different to drink in the autumn with in season fruit. Make your own Crème de Mûre – recipe at the back.

Ingredients:

- 40ml Bombay Sapphire gin
- 20ml Crème de Mûre
- 25ml lime juice
- Ginger beer
- Dash of aromatic bitters
- Blackberries

Method:

Add 5 blackberries and lime juice into mixing glass. Using a muddler press down the blackberries to bash and breakup. Add gin, Crème de Mûre and dash of aromatic bitters. Add cubed ice and stir with a bar spoon, making sure to get to bottom of glass. Top up with ginger beer and give another stir. Top up with cubed ice, add a straw and garnish with blackberry.

"Dangerously nice"

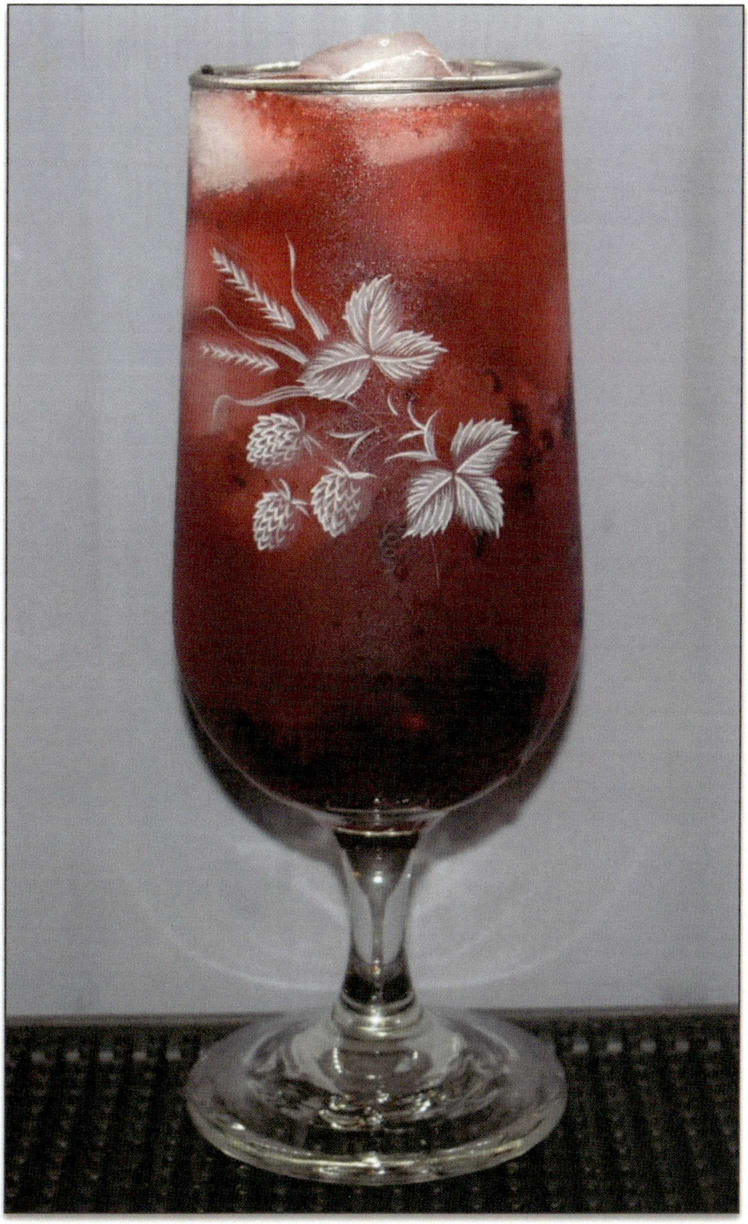

Blue Skies

This recipe was put together for our red, white and blue day, celebrating the royal wedding – just another excuse to drink on a summers Saturday afternoon to be honest.

Ingredients:

- 50ml Hortus Citrus Garden gin
- 20ml Bols Blue
- 150ml light tonic
- Lots of ice or a giant ice ball
- Blueberries to garnish

Method:

Fill a coppa glass with lots of ice. Add the gin and blue bols and mix gently. Top with tonic water and garnish with blueberries.

Tip: You can make giant balls of ice by filling small water balloons (rinse first) with water and freezing. To release the ice balls, run under hot water for a few seconds and split the balloon. You can also add a drop of natural colouring to make them more interesting.

"Great summer fruity long drink"

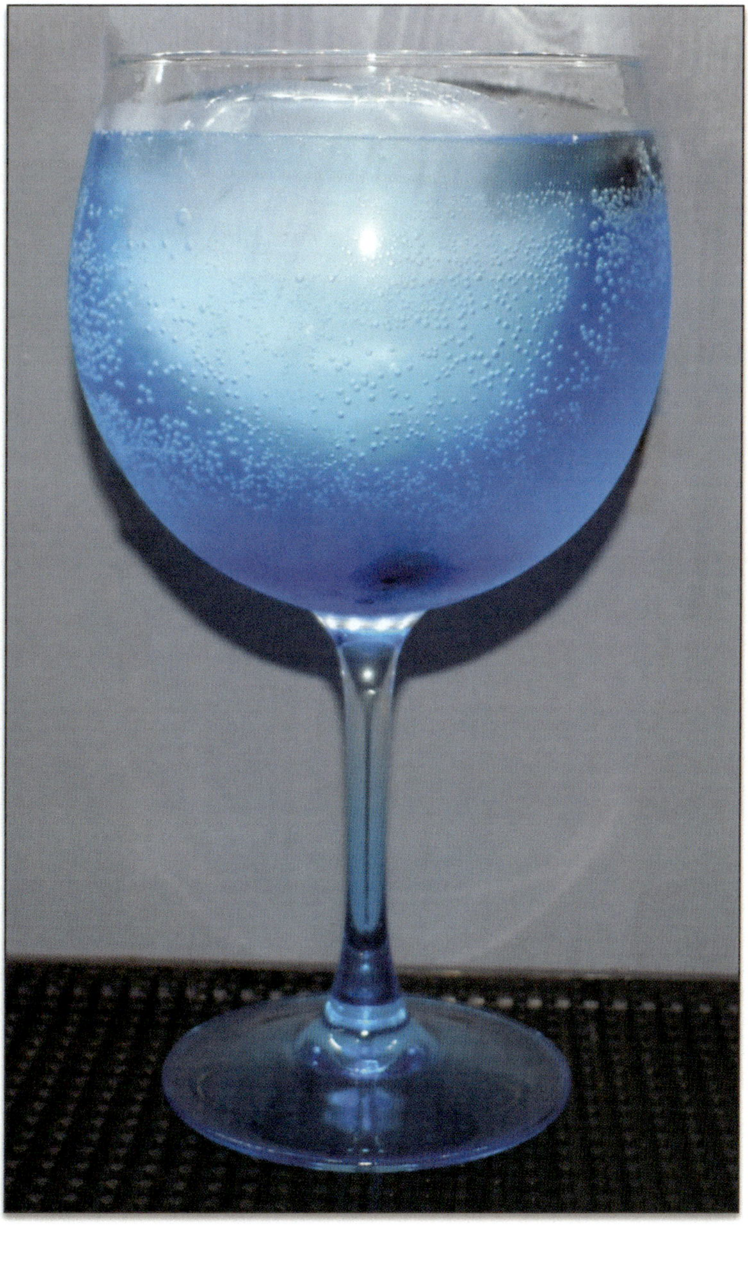

The Bramble

Definite favourite in the shed – what's not to love about a strong dark handsome drink?

Ingredients:

- 50ml Brockmans gin
- 25ml lemon juice
- 15ml Crème de Mûre
- Ice
- Slice of lemon and blackberries to garnish

Method:

Fill a rocks glass with ice ¾ of the way full. Add the gin, lemon juice and stir to mix. Garnish with the lemon slice and blackberries. Pour over the Crème de Mûre just before serving.

"Can I get that Brockmans and berry drink again, I love it"

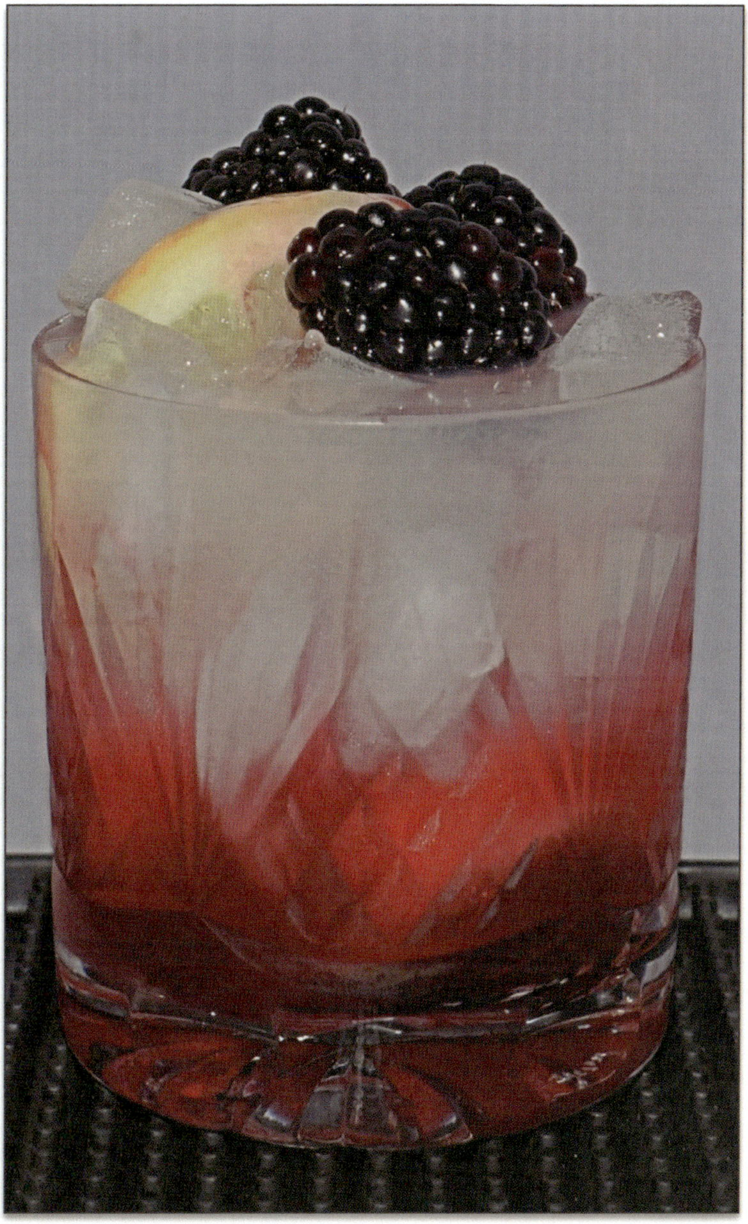

Purple Cosmo

This is not only floral, but also fruity. Nice and easy to make and drink. Great summer evening drink with a bucket of crisps on the side.

Ingredients:

- 50ml Boë Violet gin
- 40ml cranberry juice
- 10ml lime juice
- Lots of ice
- Slice of fresh lime to garnish

Method:

Add all the ingredients into mixing glass and shake to mix. Strain and pout into a chilled cocktail glass, top with the lime slice.

"The sophistication of a New York cocktail bar special but made purple for the Shed"

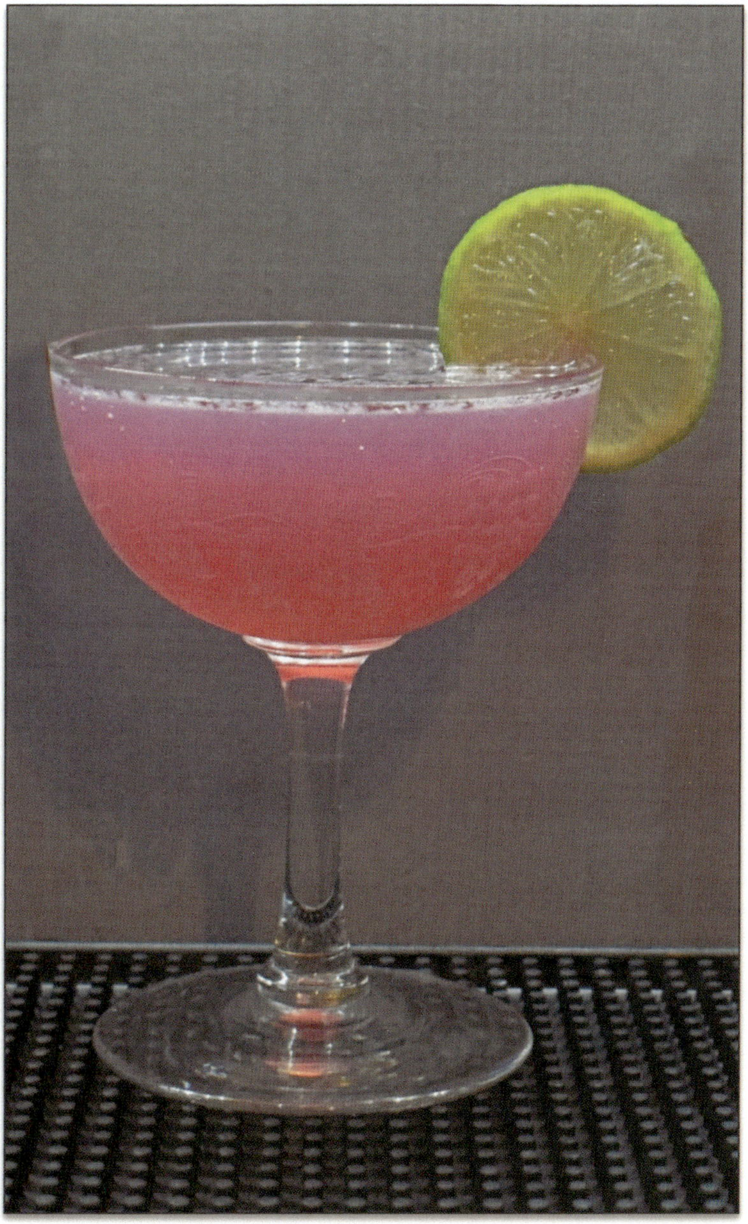

Gin Shed 22
Lime Syrup
November 2018
Gin Shed 22
Crème de Mûre
September 2018
Gin Shed 22
Fig Syrup

Recipes for stuff

This chapter is a quick intro to make your own, and why not. You can produce some great homemade infused gins using locally foraged botanicals (a botanical by the way, is a collective name for any type of plant) and combining them to suit your palette.

Syrups are also easy to make and can save money. Syrups are added to cocktails to sweeten or add fruity flavours. White sugar is the basis for most, but you can use sugar substitutes like honey, maple syrup, coconut nectar, Stevia, Agave nectar and Yacon syrup to mention a few that are widely available.

Always read the label, as some are sweeter that others and they also may have a distinctive flavour of their own which will affect the end taste of you drink.

Experiment with different fruits and herbs to make different gins or liqueurs.

If you are not feeling confident enough, there are some great gin schools out there where you can create your own gin from scratch, under the guidance of experts.

Blackberry Liqueur (Crème de Mûre)

A delicious dark fruits liqueur that is quick to make and incredibly versatile. Use instead of Kir with a champagne cocktail at Christmas or sip over ice.

Ingredients:

- 600g blackberries fresh or frozen
- 750ml bottle good-quality red wine
- 600g sugar (or sugar substitute)
- Large glass of good dry gin

Method:

Wash the blackberries and remove any stalks or leaves. Freeze over night to split skins. Tip into a large glass bowl and pour over the wine. Mash to crush the fruit into the wine. Cover with a tea towel and leave to macerate in a cool place for 2 days, mixing and mashing occasionally.

Pour the mixture through a plastic sieve, and then line a colander with a piece of muslin and sieve again to remove any bits. Tip the juice into a pan and add the sugar. Heat gently, stirring until the sugar has dissolved, then simmer for 5 minutes. Leave to cool and then stir in the gin. Using a funnel, pour into sterilised bottles, then seal and label. It's ready to use straight away. Store in a cool, dry place away from direct sunlight for up to 1 year.

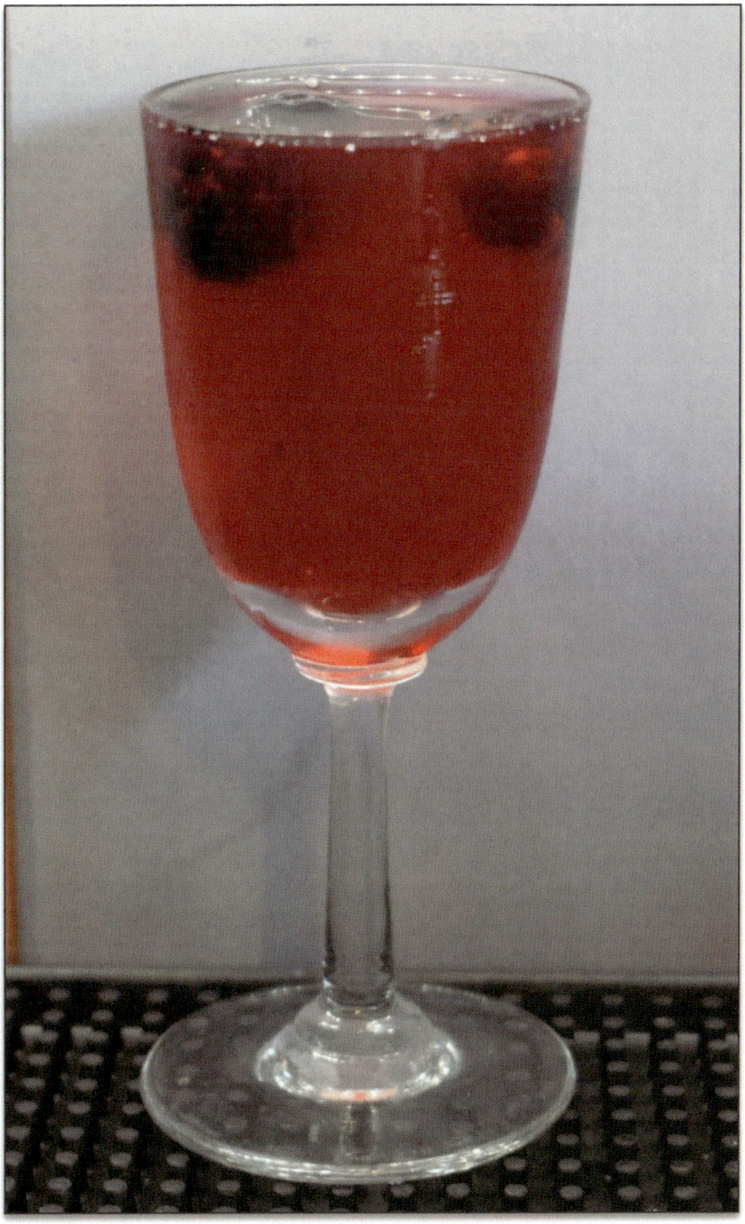

Sloe Gin

Sloe gin has been around for at least a couple of 100 years and has been used for medicinal purposes as well as cocktails. You can pick your own sloes or order on-line. There are two methods to making sloe gin – you can add the sugar at the beginning and you are likely to produce a sweet liqueur type drink. By waiting and adding dissolved sugar or substitute at the end, you can control the sweetness.

Ingredients:

- 1 litre of good quality dry gin
- 500g of ripe sloes
- Simple syrup or agave syrup or honey
- Or 250 g of sugar for traditional recipe

Method:

Freeze the sloes to split them and put in a large sterilised Kilner jar. Top with gin. Add the sugar for a traditional sloe gin liqueur (more sugar, more flavour but sweeter).

Store in a cool, dark cupboard and shake every other day for a week. Then shake once a week for a minimum of three months.

Just before you are ready to drink the sloe gin, taste test and add sweetness using a homemade simple syrup or sugar substitute like agave syrup or honey.

Strain the sloe gin through muslin into sterilised bottles and label.

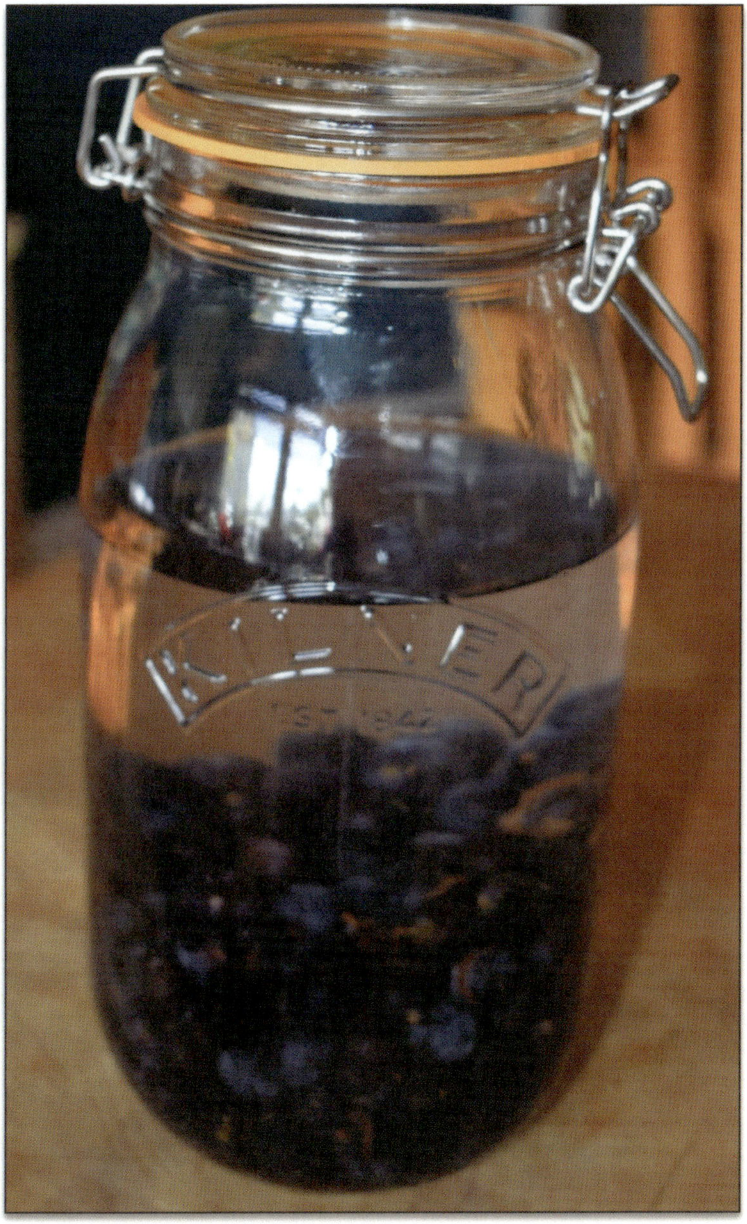
KILNER

Pink Gin

This is a basic infused red berry gin, which can easily be made at home – especially if you grow your own fruit. There are masses of pink gins readily available from supermarkets and craft gin producers, at a variety prices if you can't wait for yours to be ready.

Ingredients:

- 1 litre of good quality dry gin
- 800g of raspberries/blackberries/strawberries any combination or mix to taste – frozen can also be used
- Simple syrup or agave syrup or honey or white sugar

Method:

You will need a 2 litre Kilner jar or another glass jar or bottle that is airtight. Wash and sterilise thoroughly – or if you are using recently emptied gin bottles, there's no need to rinse.

Half fill with the gin then add washed fruit that has been previously frozen.

Store in a cool, dark cupboard and shake every other day for a week. Then shake once a week for a minimum of one month.

Just before you are ready to drink the pink gin, taste test and add sweetness using a homemade simple syrup or sugar substitute like agave syrup or honey.

Strain the pink gin through muslin into sterilised bottles and label.

Tip: You can make boozy jam from the fruit instead of throwing it away.

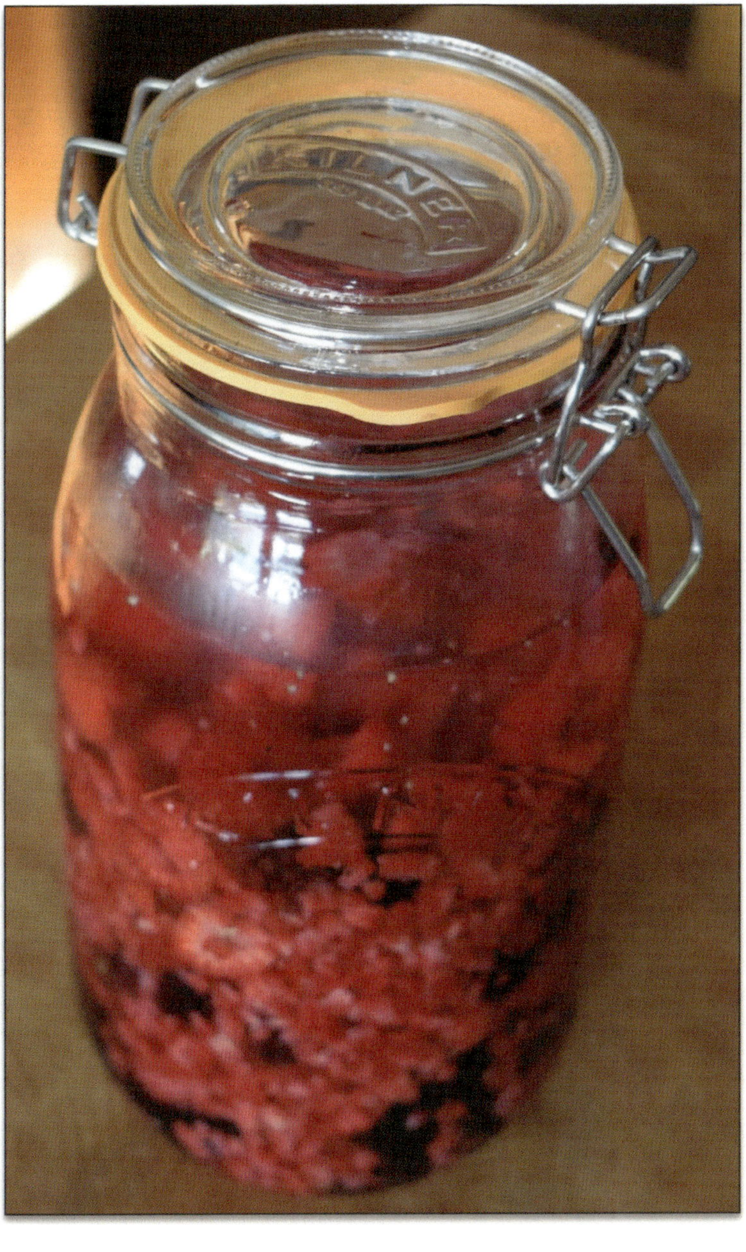

Simple Syrup

The easiest way to sweeten drinks and even your homemade gin. You can of course buy it for the nice bottle and refill with your own.

Ingredients:

- 500g white sugar
- 250ml water

Method:

Simple add the desired amount of water and sugar together into a small pan and heat gently to dissolve the sugar. Leave to cool and then add to your cocktails to sweeten when required. Store in a airtight bottle and use within 1 year.

Makes around 300ml.

Fruit syrups

Use half the above recipe and add the juice of 3 limes to create your own lime syrup.

Make with 300g of pureed raspberries for raspberry syrup – sieve to remove seeds before using.

Fig Syrup

Something a little different to normal fruit syrups, this is one is tangy and I have deliberately left the seeds in for a delicious crunch – you could use strawberries in the same way.

It is important the fruit is ripe but not bruised or going off.

Ingredients:

- 100g of washed and peeled ripe figs
- ½ lemon – juice and zest
- 100g of sugar or substitute
- 100ml of water

Method:

Chop the figs finely and add to a small pan with the water, sugar, lemon and zest.

Heat gently, stirring to mush up the figs and until the sugar is dissolved. Leave to cool, push through a fine sieve to remove any large bits of fig and lemon zest.

You should be left with pinkish syrup. You can store in a small sterilised jar or bottle and keep up to two weeks in the fridge, or freeze in an ice cube tray to be used when required. Makes about 150ml.

Shake before each use.

"FRIENDSHIP MUST BE BUILT ON A SOLID FOUNDATION OF GIN, SARCASM, INAPPROPRIATENESS & SHENANIGANS"

The Secret World of Gin Shed 22

What is Gin Shed 22? In its basic form, it is a posh garden shed, kitted out with a bar, fridge, telly, heater, sofas and a large selection of gin from around the world. What is it really? A safe place for us women to meet, rant, exchange news and ridicule our partners. We gather every few weeks, drink gin cocktails concocted by myself (although we do sometimes take turns), and snack on nibbles brought that evening. Everyone brings gin, mixers or snacks. It is an escape from the mundaneness of life. What goes on in the Gin Shed stays in the Gin Shed!

I hope you have enjoyed a glimpse into shed life from the quiet rural village of Callander in Scotland. Try some of our favourite drinks and think of us huddled in a garden shed drinking copious amounts of gin and giggling at nonsense.

Cheers

Lorraine

Acknowledgements

To the ladies of the shed, thank you for tasting my recipes, making suggestions and in many cases making tipsy comments. For your encouragement, suggestions and support. I love the group of strong women friends that we have become. Here is to many more nights in the shed with:

Jan, Jacqui, Seona, Joan, Fiona Arlene, Jenny, Dawn, Julie, Aimee, Erin and Jackie.

xox

All brands and Distillery trademarks are acknowledged.

Special Thanks to Mrs H. for help with the editing x

A note on the photography – this was done by myself in the shed, I have a squinty eye and even after editing, some of the pictures are still at an angle. It's me not you.

"I would like to personally thank all the bars I have been too and all gins I have drunk – without them, this book would not have been possible"

Lorraine Isgrove

Index

A

aromatic bitters · 58
Autumn Fruits · 40

B

Bar spoon · 8
Blackberry Liqueur · 68
Blackberry Mule · 58
Blue Skies · 60
Boë Violet Gin · 10, 22, 38, 64
Bols Blue · 60
Bombay Sapphire Gin · 10, 20, 32, 58
botanicals · 67
Breakfast Martini · 26
brine · 16
Brockmans Gin · 10, 14, 40, 62

C

Callander · 77
Champagne · 54
Citrus Gin Mojito · 36
citrus zester · 8
Classic Gin & Tonic · 32
Classic Martini · 14
Cocktail · 8
cocktail shaker · 8
coppa glass · 34
Cranberry juice · 52, 64
Crème de Mûre · 58, 62, 68

D

Dirty · 13
Dirty Martini · 16
Dry Vermouth · 24

E

elderflower tonic · 34
Equipment · 8

F

Fentimens · 31
Fever-Tree · 31
Fig Martini · 20
fig syrup · 20, 75
Floradora · 50
frozen berries · 34
Fruit syrups · 74

G

Gimlet · 28
Gin Gin Mule · 56
Gin Shed 22 · 77
ginger beer · 56, 58
Ginventory · 31
Glassware · 9
Gordon's · 31
Gordon's Gin · 18, 31

H

Hortus Citrus Garden Gin · 10, 28, 36, 60

I

Indian tonic · 42, 46

L

Lemon tonic water · 38, 44
light tonic water · 40
lime cordial · 28
lime syrup · 28, 74

M

Maraschino liqueur · 22
martini · 8, 13, 22
measures · 8

O

olives · 16
Opihr Dry Gin · 10, 16, 46, 56
orange marmalade · 26

P

Perfectly Sloe Martini · 24
Pink Gin · 11, 50, 72
Pink Gin & Tonic · 34
Pink Martini · 18
Pinkster · 11
Purple & Sweet · 38
Purple Cosmo · 64

R

raspberry syrup · 50, 74

Recipes for stuff · 67
red wine · 68

S

sieve · 8
simple syrup · 36, 56, 74
Sloe · 70
Sloe Gin · 11, 24, 44, 54, 70
Sloe Gin & Tonic · 44
Sloe Royale · 54
sloes · 70
Soda water · 36
Spanish Cosmo · 52
Spicy Nights · 46
Square Peg Pink Gin · 34
Strainer · 8
Sweet Vermouth · 24
sweeten · 74
Syrups · 67

T

Tangy Gin & Tonic · 42
Tanqueray Flor De Sevilla Gin · 11, 26, 42, 52
Tesco · 31
The Aviation · 22
The Bramble · 62
Triple sec · 52

V

Vermouth · 13, 14

Printed in Great Britain
by Amazon